세상에서 가장 가벼운 오토바이
The World's Lightest Motorcycle

이 원
Yi Won

Translated from Korean by
E. J. Koh and Marci Calabretta Cancio-Bello

Zephyr Press | Brookline, Mass

Printed in Michigan by Cushing Malloy, Inc.

Zephyr Press acknowledges with gratitude the financial support of:
The Literature Translation Institute of Korea (LTI Korea)
The Sunshik Min Endowment for the Advancement of Korean Literature
at the Korea Institute, Harvard University
The Academy of American Poets with funds from
the Amazon Literary Partnership Poetry Fund
The Massachusetts Cultural Council
The National Endowment for the Arts

Zephyr Press, a non-profit arts and education 501(c)(3) organization,
publishes literary titles that foster a deeper understanding of cultures
and languages. Zephyr Press books are distributed to the trade in the U.S.
and Canada by Consortium Book Sales and Distribution [www.cbsd.com].

Cataloguing-in publication data is available from the Library of Congress.

ISBN 978-1-938890-84-0

ZEPHYR PRESS
www.zephyrpress.org

Table of Contents

When They Ruled the Earth

The World's Lightest Motorcycle

제1부

When They Ruled the Earth

PC

—서시

'너'가 있어 호흡했던 세월의 공기를 '너'에게 다시 보낸다 내려야 할 곳을 한참 지나와버린 곳까지 끌고 와 헉헉대며 이곳에서 보낸다 끝까지 가지 못한 길의 한 모퉁이에서 놓쳐버렸던 나의 발이여 한줌의 공기여 나는 그 순간의 '나'를 눌러 그 세월을 프린트하기 시작한다 간혹 빛바랬거나 지워진 곳들도 있다 호흡을 중단했던 곳에서는 잠깐 프린트가 중단되기도 한다 그러나 심장이 그곳들을 기억한다 잠시 그 세월의 심장 속에 '나'를 담근다 캄캄한 한가운데로 시간의 커서가 내려가고 있다 온몸이 차다 숨이 막힌다 닿아야 할 그곳에 닿기 전에 기어이 종료 키를 누른다 캄캄한 모니터 화면 속으로 수평선이 무너지고 있다 그 수평선 속의 공기인 매듭을 '너'에게 보낸다

PC

—first poem

Since 'you' are here, I send years' worth of air back to 'you.' I was dragged past where I was supposed to go. Gasping for air. It's from this spot I send the air back to you. I lost my feet and my breath at the corner of the road I couldn't reach to the end. I press the 'me' from that moment to print out those years. Some parts are faded or erased. When my breath stops, the printer stops. But the heart remembers those parts. I soak 'me' in the heart of those years. The cursor of time falls in the thick of darkness. My body is cold, my breath is blocked. Press the 'end' key before it reaches its destination. The horizon collapses into the dark monitor screen. I send 'you' a knot of air from that horizon.

거리에서

내 몸의 사방에 플러그가
빠져나와 있다
탯줄 같은 그 플러그들을 매단 채
문을 열고 밖으로 나온다
비린 공기가
플러그 끝에 주렁주렁 매달려 있다
곳곳에서 사람들이
몸 밖에 플러그를 덜렁거리며 걸어간다
세계와의 불화가 에너지인 사람들
사이로 공기를 덧입은 돌들이
둥둥 떠다닌다

On the Street

Plugs are unthreading
from every part of my body
suspended like umbilical cords
I open the door and go outside
Foul air
clusters at the end of each plug
People everywhere
walk with plugs suspended from their bodies
charged by the world's rage
In the spaces between them
pebbles clothed in the air float buoyantly

그림자

숨막히는 한낮의 아스팔트를 끌며 검은 그림자 하나가 간다
그림자 디지털 시계처럼 고요하다
떠나온 곳을 알 수 없는 한떼의 공기
주전자의 보리차처럼 그림자에게 쏟아져내린다

비린 살육의 냄새
(동물이었구나)

Shadow

Dragging the asphalt on a sweltering midday one dark
            shadow passes along
The shadow is quiet like a digital clock
A swarm of air appears from some unknown place
pours over the shadow like barley tea from a kettle

The reek of slaughter
(So it was an animal)

시간과 비닐 봉지

검은, 비닐 봉지 하나, 길바닥을 굴러다닌다 계속해서 시간은, 길보다 먼저 다리를 뻗는다, 검은 비닐 봉지, 이번에는 계단이 있는 곳까지, 굴러가더니 멈춘다 잠시 따갑게, 부스럭거린다 시간은 다리를, 양 옆으로 길을 벌리며 간다, 가다 간판, 밑에서 멈춘다 무방비 상태로 옷의 앞을 모두, 풀어놓은 채 시간은 계속되고, 있다며 비닐 봉지, 검은 쓰레기가 있는 곳으로 굴러 들어간다, 한참 나오질 않더니 검은, 그림자를 흔들며 헤집으며, 나무 밑에 멈춰 있다, 그곳에서 시간과, 비닐 봉지가 같은 색으로 만난다, 나무에 등을, 기댄 시간의 한쪽 다리가 무릎에서, 잘려 있다 뒤를 보니 나무의, 중간쯤에 다리를 접어 올리고, 있다 비닐 봉지는 여전히, 나무 밑에 머물러 있고 몸을 앞으로, 숙인 시간은 무엇인가를 뒤로, 껴안고 있다

Time and a Plastic Bag

One, black plastic bag, rolls over the road, time constantly, stretches its legs ahead, of the road, now the plastic bag, rolls toward the stairs, and stops, rustling, and pricked for a moment, time straddles on, both sides of the road, as it goes, stopped at the bottom of an advertisement, sign, time keeps on, helplessly, with its clothes unbuttoned, at the front, the plastic bag, rolls into a dark pile of trash, it stays longer, then its shadow moves, digging toward a tree where it stops, here, time and the plastic bag meet, the same color, time leans against the tree, with one leg cut off, at the knee, looking again, time had just folded its leg against the middle of the tree, the plastic bag stays single-minded, under this tree as time bows forward, embracing something, behind its back.

철, 킥, 철, 킥

의자에 앉아, 그녀는, 현관문을 바라본다 닫혀진, 세계의 문 밑에서 소리없이 그림자가 멈춘다, 멈춘, 그림자가 세계를 덮친다 사라진, 세계 위로, 그림자가 움직인다 그녀는, 꼼짝 않고 그림자를, 쳐다본다, 철, 킥, 하는 소리가, 나더니 그림자가 없어진다, 계속해서, 그녀는 현관문을, 바라보며 컵에 물을, 따른다 세계가, 출렁, 거린다, 물소리는 텅 빈 길을 가지고 있다, 세계는 컵의 바깥으로 흘러내리기도, 한다 갑자기 급브레이크 밟는 소리, 컵을 강타한다 그녀는 침대에, 주저앉는다, 들춰진 이불 밑에 시간의 옷자락이 구겨져 있다, 그녀는, 한 손으로 이불을, 쓰다듬으며 현관문을 쳐다본다 가느다란, 빛이 들어오던 세계의 문, 밑으로 또다시 그림자가 드리운다, 점점 더 깊숙이 들어온다 방안이, 어두워진다 컵이 바싹, 마르며 타들어간다, 그녀는 수도꼭지를 튼다, 그 안에 끼였던, 세계가 쏟아진다, 세계는 그녀에게도, 튄다, 순식간에 세계를 껴입은 그녀, 손을 뻗어 시계를, 찾는다 손목시계가 석간신문 밑에 깔려 있다, 그녀는, 문의 세계의 잠금쇠를, 쳐다보며 시계를, 쳐든다 세계, 안에서 디지털 시계가 철, 킥, 철, 킥, 사물이 없는 텅 빈, 시간 속을 가고 있다

Tick, Tick, Tick, Tick

She, sits in a chair, stares at the closed front door, from beneath the world's, door the shadow noiselessly pauses, halts, the shadow strikes the vanishing, world the shadow moves, she, stays still, stares at the shadow, tick, tick, the shadow disappears, she, continues to stare at the door, pours water into a cup, the world sloshes, there's an empty road inside the sloshing sound, the world spills over, the side of the cup, suddenly the sound of screeching brakes, she throws the cup hard, she flops down, on her bed, time's crinkled hem under the blanket, she, strokes the blanket, while staring at the door, a thin ray of light seeps through the world's door, the shadow enters again from beneath, little by little coming further into the room, the room darkens, the cup dries up to the point of combusting, she turns on the faucet, the world jammed up, inside the faucet, gushes out, the world splatters over her too, in an instant, she's wearing layers of the world she, stretches out her hand, she searches for her wristwatch, she, finds it buried beneath the evening paper, she stares at the lock on the world's door, as she picks up her watch, inside the world, the digital wristwatch ticks, ticks, ticks, ticks, the watch is moving, inside time's hollow world.

책

책에는 시계가 붙어 있다 시계에 초침은 없다 가만히 보면 시계는 언제나 한 곳에 머물고 있다 사람들이 세계를 떠메고 쉴새없이 달린다 그 발자국을 시간이라 부른다 부른다는 듯이 책에 시간이 정지되어 있다 아직은 인간의 냄새가 배어 있지 않은 그러나 예정된 시간의 발자국 같은 발자국이 감추고 있는 웅성거림 같은 웅성거림 안에 스며 있는 숨소리 같은 숨들이 몰고 오는...........

Book

A clock is stuck to a book, the clock has no second hand, looking more closely the clock hesitates at one fixed point, people shoulder the world, constantly running, their footprints we call time, time stops in a book, the human scent has not soaked through, but like the foreseeable footprints of time, like the footprint hiding its hum, like the sound of a breath permeating inside that hum, breaths are herded in . . .

발자국은 신발을 닮았다

발을 넣으려는 순간 왈칵 어두운
현관의 두 짝 신발이 축축하게
제 몸을 다 벌리고 있다
허공에 있던 발을
내리고 주저앉으니
공기의 냄새가 비어 있다
신발 안을 들여다본다 꾹꾹
몸이 걸었으므로 길이 되어버린
마음이 우글우글하다
신발을 굽어보던 빈 몸이
뻣뻣해 벽에 몸을 기댄다
길이 되지 못한 벽이 움찔거려
기댄 벽이 무겁다 세계의
어디서나 출입구는
입과 항문처럼 뚫려 있다
두 발로 단단한 바닥을
딛으며 다시 일어선다
(새삼 발자국은 신발을 닮았다!)
신발 속으로 현실의 발을 집어넣는다
그 속은 아득하고 둥글다
한 발을 살짝 문밖으로 내민다
덥썩 세계의 입이 닫힌다

Footprints Are Like Shoes

Soon as I slip my feet inside
a pair of shoes their damp body
opens wide across a dark corridor
and hovering feet sit down
The scent of the air is empty
I peek into my shoes
My body walks rigidly
My heart, as a road, swarms
My empty body that overlooks
the shoes stiffens against a wall
The wall that couldn't be a road
winces. The wall that's leaned on
feels heavy. Entrances are open
anywhere in the world
like a mouth or anus
I step onto hard ground
standing again on two feet
(new footprints are like shoes!)
Slipping the feet of reality inside
it feels unfamiliar and round
One foot slips out the door
The mouth of the world closes

봄 • 편지

봄이다 라고 적자마자 그 (봄) 안으로 나비가 날아든다 유리창 속에서 밥그릇 속에서 시계 속에서 접혀진 무릎 속에서 못 속에서도 나비가 튀어나온다 날개가 없는 것도 나비라는 이름으로 모여든다 하늘을 담은 유리창으로 물고기들이 날개를 달고 오기도 한다 손에 무엇인가를 들고 오는 나비도 있다 그 중에는 오래 전에 내가 그에게 보낸 석 줄의 편지도 있다 내가 보낸 구절 중 죽었나?가 죽었다로 고쳐져 있다 물음표를 검게 지운 자리에

Spring • Letter

As I write it's spring, a butterfly flutters in (spring). From the glass window, from a rice bowl, from a clock, from folded knees, even from a nail, butterflies flutter out. Even wingless things gather in the name of butterflies. Fish with wings arrive through the glass window filled with sky. Certain butterflies bring in what they collect on their legs. Among them, three lines of a letter I sent him long ago. Among these lines, *Are you dead?*—has changed to *I am dead* marked with a black smear.

엽서

마악 너의 주소를 적어넣으려 하고
있어 오늘의 공기는 딱딱해
너의 이름과 주소를
적어넣을 때 창가의 수선화가
제 우주를 마악 열지도 몰라 그럼
열린 수선화 속에 너의
이름과 주소를 빠트릴 거야
너의 이름과 주소에서는
온통 수선화의 우주가 만져지겠지
공기도 리듬의 붕대를 풀 거야

엽서의 오른쪽 구석에서
목에 동그란 방울 두 개를 단
고양이가 마악 초록 눈을 뜨고 있어
오늘을 팽팽하게
감각하고 있는 눈이야 빛나는 털은
안테나처럼 사방을 잡아당기고
수염은 몸 밖 멀리 뻗고 있어
그 고양이의 초록 눈 아래
너의 이름을 적었어 날숨 속에서
너의 이름이 보드랍게 빛났어

Postcard

I'm writing down your address
Today the air is brittle
As I write down your name and address
the daffodils by the window
open up their universe
I'm dropping your name
into the open daffodils
I can touch the cosmos of the daffodils
in your address
Air loosens the bandage of rhythm

In the right corner of the postcard
a cat with two round bells on its neck
is opening its green eyes
Like an antenna
the cat's shiny coat and observing eyes
pull at the day in all directions
like whiskers sticking out all over
I write down your name
beneath the cat's green eyes
Your name gleams

너의 주소를 꿈틀꿈틀 이어 적고
여섯 개의 빈 사각에
고양이의 발자국 같은 우편번호를
적었어 사각이 출렁거려
셋째 칸의 숫자가 사각을
비집고 나가 이탈한 꼬리를 따라
사각 끝이 툭툭 터지고 있어
6개의 또 다른 빈 사각은
고양이와 마주보는 곳에 매달렸지
사각 안을 채우지는 않을 거야
내가 그곳에 있어
들고 있는 만년필에서 잉크가
뚝 열매처럼 떨어졌어

공기의 귀가 떨어져나가 사방에서
바람이 몰려들고 있어
문들이 덜컹거려 자꾸 잉크가 번져
너의 이름과 주소들이
우글거려 시간이 엉키고 공기가
버석거려 쪼개도 쪼개도 공기의 속은
말갛다고 숨이 막혀
너에게 새파란 그림자가
다가오고 있어 그러나 결코
그 무엇도 너를 관통할 수는 없어
쓰라린 흙처럼 내가 너를 덮어

I scrawl your address
inside the six blank boxes
I write your zip code like
a cat's pawprint. The boxes waver
The third number pushes its way out
of its box and rolls along the tail
The edges of the boxes break apart
Six more blank boxes in a different square
dangle facing the cat
That's where I am
The ink of my fountain pen
drops like fruit

The air's ears fall off
The wind pours in from everywhere
The doors rattle and the ink keeps spreading
Your name and address
crowd in. Time entangles and air rustles
No matter how much I split and split
the air is clear and makes me gasp for breath
A blue shadow approaches
but nothing
can pass through you
I cover you like bitter soil

당신의 소포

보내주신 소포 잘 받았습니다
집으로 오르는 계단은 모두 지워져 있었습니다
좁은 복도는 벼랑처럼 아득했습니다
당신이 보내신 소포는 왜 그리 가벼운지요
문신 같은 초생달이 떠올랐습니다
하늘은 더 이상 물러설 곳이 없는 거울 속 같았습니다
밤의 등을 켜든 창이 잠깐 빛났습니다
마분지를 살그머니 벗겼습니다
창이 숨을 자꾸 놓쳤습니다 그러나
벗겨도 벗겨도 세월의 붕대 같은 마분지만 보였습니다
마분지 위를 쓰다듬어보면
여전히 사각의 딱딱한 통이 만져졌습니다
아아 무덤이 그렇게 따뜻하리라고는 생각하지 않았습니다

Your Package

Thank you for the package
Every stair to the house is erased
The long corridor as narrow as a cliff
Why is your package so light?
The tattoo-like crescent moon rises
The sky as shallow as a mirror
At night I turn on the light, the window beams
I discreetly peel off the wrapping paper
The window skips a breath
I peel and peel the paper but only see time's bandage
When I caress the package
I can feel its hard edges
Ah! I didn't think a coffin could be so warm

공기에게

조금만 더 안으로 밀고
들어와줄 수는 없겠니
들어와 숨막히게 아니 몸막히게

To the Air

Can't you please
press in a bit more?
Enter so my breath stops, no, so my body chokes

길 또는 그물

길은 그물이다 몸을 가진 것들은 걸린다 걸려본 발이 길을 알리라 길 가운데 선 청동의 동상에도 그물의 그림자가 비친다 허리에 찬 위풍당당한 칼도 예외는 아니다 공기가 포장지처럼 바스락거린다 길 밖의 키 작은 채송화는 다른 길을 만든다 간간히 꽃망울 잎망울까지도 물과 흙을 담은 길이다 길의 무너지는 무덤들이 꽃 속으로 스며든다 이파리와 이파리 사이에서 조금씩 벌어지는 하늘이 새하얗게 바랜다 공기는 얼룩이 져 있다 어김없이 하늘을 따라가는 길 가파른 매듭을 보여주고 매듭은 깊은 골짜기를 몰고 온다 높은 곳의 웅덩이에서 몇 개의 자루를 지고 가는 구름 구름 속으로 지상의 그물이 삭아내린다

Road or Net

The road is a net. Corporeal things get caught. Tripping feet know the way. The bronze statue in the middle of the road reflects the net's shadow. Even a majestic sword strapped at the waist is no exception. The air rustles like wrapping paper. From the road, the smallest moss rose makes a different road. It's a road that leads water and soil to the tips of its leaves and flowers. Crumbling graves permeate the flowers. The sliver of sky between leaf and leaf looks pale. The mottled air. The road following the sky reveals a steeply intricate knot herding through a deep valley of precipitation. Inside this high bog, clouds carrying sacks of moisture dissipate into the earth's net.

재크의 콩나무

지하1층 식품 매장 재크가 엘리베이터를 타고 있습니다
　　　(엘리베이터의 ↑ 속에 뿌리가 자라고 있습니다)
1 층 신변 잡화 매장을 지나 재크는 올라갑니다
　　　(엘리베이터의 ↑ 속에 뿌리가 자라고 있습니다)
2 층 숙녀 의류 매장을 지나 재크는 올라갑니다
　　　(엘리베이터의 ↑ 속에 뿌리가 자라고 있습니다)
3 층 신사 의류 매장을 지나 재크는 올라갑니다
　　　(엘리베이터의 ↑ 속에 뿌리가 자라고 있습니다)
4 층 아동 의류매장을 지나 재크는 올라갑니다
　　　(엘리베이터의 ↑ 속에 뿌리가 자라고 있습니다)
5 층 가전 제품 매장을 지나 재크는 올라갑니다
　　　(엘리베이터의 ↑ 속에 뿌리가 자라고 있습니다)
6 층 주방용품 매장을 지나 재크는 올라갑니다
　　　(엘리베이터의 ↑ 속에 뿌리가 자라고 있습니다)
7 층 침구 매장을 지나 재크는 올라갑니다
　　　(엘리베이터의 ↑ 속에 뿌리가 자라고 있습니다)
8 층 스카이라운지 매장을 지나 재크는 올라갑니다
　　　(엘리베이터의 ↑ 속에 뿌리가 자라고 있습니다)
엘리베이터의 ↑ 속에 자라고 있는 뿌리는
하늘 아래 모든 埋葬 으로 통합니다

Jack's Beanstalk

Jack rides the elevator to the first floor of the grocery store
  (In the elevator roots are growing ↑)
Jack comes up through the 1st floor personal goods
  (In the elevator roots are growing ↑)
Jack comes up through the 2nd floor women's clothing
  (In the elevator roots are growing ↑)
Jack comes up through the 3rd floor men's clothing
  (In the elevator roots are growing ↑)
Jack comes up through the 4th floor children's clothing
  (In the elevator roots are growing ↑)
Jack comes up through the 5th floor home appliances
  (In the elevator roots are growing ↑)
Jack comes up through the 6th floor kitchen utensils
  (In the elevator roots are growing ↑)
Jack comes up through the 7th floor bedroom furniture
  (In the elevator roots are growing ↑)
Jack comes up through the 8th floor Sky Lounge
  (In the elevator roots are growing ↑)
The roots growing inside the elevator are connected
to the buried corpses under heaven

밥그릇과 그림자 사이

시간

펑, 아스팔트 위에서 타이어 터지는 소리가 들린다. 길은 한 순간에 구겨진다. 구겨진 길을 덮치는 새떼들. 새떼들이 펑 소리를 뒤덮어 숨막힐 때 내 식탁 귀퉁이에 놓여 있던 밥그릇의 한쪽이 들린다. 그림자는 여전히 구겨진 세계에 붙어 있다. 비어 있는 밥그릇, 물방울은 떨어지다 멈춰 있고 시간은 더 깊게 비어간다. 만져보면 차갑게 멈춰 있는 밥그릇과 그림자 사이, 점점 길 끝으로 가파르게 지워지는

부채

빚이 늘어간다. 동쪽의 죄가 늘어간다. 해는 죄에서 떠오른다. 손이 온통 썰렁하다. 버리지 못한 편지 봉투가 책상 위에서 혼자 펄럭인다. 비가 샜던 벽에 유난히 얼룩이 진다. 이런 날은 짜장면을 시켜 먹는다. 전화벨이 짜장면 가락처럼 시커멓게 울린다. 나는 받지 않는다. 계속해서 전화벨이 쌓인다. 아버지의 상여를 뒤따를 때 날 두들기던 요령 소리. 동그란 핏줄이 칼처럼 날카롭다. 피는 부채 탕감이냐. 나는 피냄새를 맡으며 뭉클하다

Between a Rice Bowl and Shadow

Time

POP! Over the asphalt I hear a tire popping. Within a few seconds the road is mangled. Birds cover the torn up road. When I hear the birds, I grow breathless and the edge of my rice bowl lifts from the corner of my dinner table. Shadows stick to the wrecked world. Rice bowls empty, water stops dripping, time deepens. If you touch between the cooling rice bowl and shadow, more and more of the road's end is steeply erased.

Debt

Debt grows. Guilt grows in the east. The sun rises from guilt. My hands grow cold. An empty envelope flutters, undiscarded, alone on the desk. Because there's a leak, the rain stains the wall. On a day like this, I order a noodle dish with black bean sauce. The phone rings like noodles drenched in black bean sauce. I don't answer. The ringing piles up. When I walked behind my father's casket, the sound of the wooden bell beat against me. A round vein is as sharp as a knife. Does blood forgive debt? I am moved by the smell of blood.

내용

벽에 있던 거울을 떼서 TV 위에 올려놓는다. TV 위에 거울, 거울 옆에
달려 있는 달력, 달력 속의 폴 고갱의 그림. 거울 한쪽 구석에 붙어 있는
턱을 괴고 앉아 있는 꼬마 아이. 그 꼬마 아이를 떼내고, 5월에 머물러 있
는 폴 고갱의 그림을 한 장 찢고 한쪽이 부러진 TV 실내 안테나의 다른
한쪽도 마저 망가뜨리는 것. 그것이 내가 오늘 중으로 해야 할 일이다. 집
안 곳곳에 올려져 있거나 쌓여져 있는 상자와 보따리들. 이고 강을 건너
야 한다. 내용물은 솜이다

Content

I take the mirror from a wall and place it over the TV. Mirror above the TV, the calendar hanging next to the mirror, Paul Gauguin's painting on the calendar. In one corner of the mirror a small child sits holding his chin. I rip out the child, Paul Gauguin's painting in May, and break off one side of the TV antenna, which is already broken on the other side. I need to finish this by midday. Boxes and bags are stacked inside my house. I need to carry them across the river on my back. The contents are just stuffing.

옷걸이와 남방셔츠

못의, 날카로운 끝이 존재의 어디를 찌르고, 있는지는 알 수가 없다, 다만 찬 못에 흰, 옷걸이의 모가지가, 물음표처럼 살짝, 그러나 분명하게 걸려 있다 (존재의 저 단호한 의문문!) 옷걸이의 모가지의 동서 경제 블록으로는, 남방의 생이, 늘어져 있다 남방은, 벽에서 이데올로기처럼 시들어도, 존재의 순결의 옷걸이의 물음표는, 여전히 확고하고, 둥글게 화해의 제스처와 해방의 신호를 내보이는, 못과 그 아래서 남방의 옷깃은 짝짝이다, 동쪽이 아래로 축, 늘어져 가파른, 내리막길이다 그러나, 동과, 서의, 벌어진 간격을 좁힐 기구가, 이곳에는 마련되어 있지 않다, 동서의 신화는 이미 죽었다, 지금 권력은 회귀성을 띤다 마찬가지다, 남방의 오른팔은, 옷 안으로 깊숙하게 들어와 있고, 왼팔은 아예, 옷 밖으로 나가버렸다, 동서의 밖이, 문득 당당하다고 느닷없이, 바람이 불어닥칠 때마다 옷 밖으로 나간 왼팔이, 그림자를 휘젓는다 그래도, 회귀하지 않는 것은 오로지, 남방의 어깨, 남방의 어깨만은 확고한 선을, 가지고 있다 남방의 어깨는, 옷걸이의, 존재의, 하얀 뼈다.

Shirt and Hanger

Nail, the sharp edge of a nail is piercing existence, I don't know where, the cold nail, hanger's neck, like a question mark, but clearly hanging (that resolute question of existence!) the hanger is the east-west, shirt, a drooping shirt, wilting on the wall like an ideology, the question of the hanger of the purity of existence, is unyielding, showing a roundabout conciliatory gesture and sign of liberation, below the nail and collar are mismatched, drooping on the eastern axis, a sheer drop, at this point no mechanism can narrow the gap between east and west, the myth of east and west is already dead, now the power is showing signs of regression, nothing has changed, the shirt's right arm is tucked deep inside, the left arm has practically slipped out, outside of the east-west, the left arm flutters confidently each time the wind blows, stirring the clouds, but the one thing that hasn't regressed is the shirt's shoulder, the one thing retaining a definite line, the shirt's shoulder is the white hanger's existence, white bone.

냉장고 앞에서

냉장고 앞에 섰다
속을 알 수 없는

1. 배후에서 어딘가로 줄이 이어지고 있다 과거와 미래가 존재한다
2. 침묵을 비집고 가끔씩 윙윙 소리가 난다 현재가 여기 있다
3. 완강한 몸 위에 늘 은밀한 불을 켜들고 있다 실존이 사실이다

역사 앞에 섰다
속을 알 수 없는
스스로 열지 않으면 열리지 않는

안으로부터 시간의 반죽이
썩어가고 있을 역사 앞에 섰다

Before the Refrigerator

I stand before the refrigerator
the unknowable

1. Behind me a line exists between the past and future
2. The present opens the silence and hums. The present exists here
3. Existence holds up a secret light above a sturdy body. Existence is truth

I stand before history
the unknowable
If history doesn't open itself, it won't open

From within, the dough of time
stands before the rotting of history

모래 무덤

아이들이 모래 무덤을 만들고 있다
한 손을 가운데 넣고 모래를 수북이 쌓고 꾹꾹 누른다
막대기를 가운데 넣고 모래를 수북이 쌓고 꾹꾹 누른다
세상은 뼈와 살이 다져진 곳이라는 듯이 꾹꾹 누른다
제 몸을 동그랗게 말고 있는 아이들의 엉덩이가 무덤 같은데

아이들은 막대기를 묻고 막대기를 궁금해한다
아이들은 제 손을 묻고 제 손을 궁금해한다

Sand Grave

Children are building sand graves
With one hand in the middle, they cover it up with sand,
                      press, weigh it down
A stick in the middle, they cover it up with sand, press,
                      weigh it down
The world as chopped bones and flesh, press, weigh it down
Children roll themselves into balls, their buttocks are graves

Children bury the stick and wonder
Children bury their hands and wonder

청량리 정신병원 근처

허겁지겁 불이 바뀌고 철문이 닫히고 녹슨 세월이 닫힌다

문득 세상 쪽으로 거무칙칙한 그림자와

입간판 위로 드리워진 그늘이 소리를 숨기고

풀밭에 주저앉아 있는 풀들은 세상의 모든 길들이 그립다

나무가 비의처럼 숨겨놓은 물이 가끔 후두둑 소리를 안고 땅으로 떨어진다

내려앉던 안개가 높은 담을 둘러싸고

쇠창살 밖을 기웃거리는 목 늘어진 유행가에 맞추어

미주아파트 입구를 빠져나온 오후반 아이들

장화를 신고 첨벙첨벙 담장 높은 학교로 간다

By Cheongnyang-ni Mental Hospital

The lights change quickly, the iron gate shuts with rusted years

then over the side of the world a murky shadow

and the shade over the billboard hides its sound

Grass sitting on grass yearns for the roads of the world

The water hidden by trees sometimes carries dripping sounds
and falls to the ground

The seated fog circles the high wall of the hospital

The afternoon class of children spills out of the apartment lobby

bobbing their heads to music beyond the window's metal bars

Their boots splash and patter toward their school with high walls

너는 어디에서 왔으며, 무엇이며, 어디로 가는가

골목 끝에 집이 있다
집이 그늘이다
나는 어제의 집에 그늘로 앉는다
공기가 육친처럼 불편하다
아이들이 그러나 세월처럼 지나간다

지금
시간처럼
공기처럼
너는

Where You Come From, What You Are, Where You're Going

Your house is at the end of an alley
Your house is shade
I sit in the shade of yesterday's house
The air is cumbersome like family
Children, however, pass like years

Now
you are
like time
like air

풍경의 끝

창은 창으로 남아 있어야 한다, 그 창에는 양쪽으로 드리워진 커튼이 있고 무수한 별들이 일사불란하게 떴다 지고 다시 뜨고 있었다. 그 아래, 한 남자와 한 여자가 탁자를 사이에 두고 마주앉았다

등불이 그 남자와 그 여자 사이를 가르며 매달려 있다. 머리 위의 등불의 존재를 알지 못하는 것은 지금 탁자 위에서 급작스럽게 손을 맞잡은 그 남자와 그 여자뿐이었다. 저쪽을 봐, 남자가 여자를 풀어주듯 몸을 의자에 기댄다. 손은 서로 붙잡고 있다. 여자가 고개를 돌려 남자가 가리키는 방향을 쳐다본다. 저쪽을 봐, 남자는 자꾸 함께 붙잡은 손을 자기 쪽으로 끌어당긴다. 여자도 남자가 가리키는 쪽을 보며 자기 쪽으로 당기며 그리고 서로 밀리고 있다. 자꾸만 벌리는 그 여자와 남자의 컴컴한 입 속으로 별들이 구른다. 입을 닫으면 별들이 사라진다. 우주는 그렇게 쉽게 열리고 닫히고 있었다. ㅈ ㅉ ㅇ ㅂ ㅇ 남자의 말이 여자에게로 가기도 전에 허공에서 뚝뚝 끊어지고 그 순간 우루루 별들이 쏟아졌다. 등불이 탁자 위에 떨어진 별들을 비추었다. 별들이 잠깐 새까매진다

창은 차갑게 비추고 있다. 여전히 한 남자와 한 여자가 앉아 있다. 그래, 그 창의 한가운데 놓인 촛불만이 짐승처럼 아름다운 그 때 창이 보여주는 풍경, 풍경의 끝 한 순간, 그 남자와, 그 여자가, 블랙홀 속으로, 빨려, 들어간다

The Landscape's End

The window must stay a window, draped with curtains on either side, countless stars perfectly appear and disappear. Beneath them, a man and woman sit across a table.

A lamp hangs between them. Oblivious to the light overhead, they suddenly clasp their hands across the table. Look, the man leans back as if letting go of the woman. But their hands are clasped. She looks over to where he's pointing. She pulls him toward her, and they get yanked around. The stars inside their opened dark mouths are rolling. If they close their mouths, the stars will vanish. The universe opens and closes so easily. Z. ZZ. O. B. O . . . Before his letters reach the woman, they split apart in mid-air. Then the stars shower over them. The lamp shines on fallen stars across the table. The stars darken.

The window glows coldly. The man and woman stay seated. The time when just the candle at the center of the window was as pretty as an animal . . . the end of the landscape . . . in an instant, the man, and woman, are sucked, into, a black hole.

환한 방

거울 속에 녹슨 기적 소리들이 쌓인다
거울 속에 구부러진 길들이 이리저리 쌓인다
짐을 끄는 낙타들의 발자국이 찍힌다
거울 속에 낯선 유리창이 쌓인다
거울 속에 아직도 모양이 남아 있는 것들이 이리저리 쌓인다
거울 속에 두 손으로 거리의 열쇠를 쥐고
정처없이 어둑어둑해지는 서쪽 하늘이 몸을 쪼그리며 쌓인다
거울 속에 더 이상 어두워질래야 어두워질 수 없는 곳
그곳에서까지 껌벅거리던 별들이 여전히 뒹군다
거울 속에 험하고 투명한 골짜기가 여기저기 패인다

A Bright Room

In the mirror the sound of rusted whistles piles up
In the mirror bent roads from everywhere pile up
Camel hoofprints hauling loads
In the mirror windows I've never seen pile up
In the mirror things that still have shapes pile up
In the mirror hands carry a key to the road
The aimlessly dim sky squats down, piling up
In the mirror there's a place that can't get any darker
In this place the blinking stars keep rolling around
In the mirror jagged transparent valleys cave in

제2부

The World's Lightest Motorcycle

자화상

머리를 일산 시장 좌판에 내놓았는데 며칠이 지나도 사가는 사람이 없다

머리를 옥션 경매에 올렸는데 클릭을 해도 머리에서 모래시계가 생겨나지 않는다는 연락이 왔다

머리를 벼룩시장 난전에 가져갔더니 대뜸 풍선처럼 불어본다 쭈글쭈글한 머리가 조금씩 펴지고 입이 벌어진다 남의 지문을 씹고 있는 입은 다행히 아직 울부짖지는 않는다

Self-Portrait

I put my head on display at Ilsan Market, but after several days no one bought it

I put my head up for auction online but got a notification that when you click my head an hourglass appears, a loading error

I take my head to a flea market, but somebody blows it up like a balloon and my wrinkled head gradually smooths out and my mouth chews on somebody else's fingerprints and to my great relief my mouth has yet to howl

주유소의 밤

남자가 여자의 왼쪽 옆구리를 뜯어내 주유기를 걸쳐 놓고 한 손으로
는 여자의 목을 또 한 손으로는 여자의 머리를 쓰다듬고 있다

여자가 남자의 배를 뜯어내고 밀어넣은 주유기를 두손으로 잡은 채
쉴 새 없이 깔깔거리고 있다

남자가 남자의 등을 뜯어내고 그러고는 담배에 불을 붙이고 있다 주
유기는 뼈 사이에 걸려 있다

세상의 모든 차들은 휘발되는 불빛을 믿고 길을 만들고

의외로 간단한 조합인 남자와 남자 또는 여자와 남자 또는 여자와 여
자는 몸만 바꾸고

A Night at the Gas Station

The man rips off the woman's left torso, lifts the hose and pumps gas. With his other hand, he strokes her neck and hair

She rips out the man's belly, and seizing the pump, starts to giggle nonstop

The man rips out his spine, then lights up a cigarette. The pump is left dangling between his bones

All the cars in the world trust the traffic signal and make a road

of unexpected bodies switching between man and man or woman and man or woman and woman

집은 여행 중

이중창과 방범창까지 닫힌 집 속에서 길 하나가
탈장처럼 빠져나온다
그 길 속에서 타다 만 사내와 개가 미끄러져 나온다
성기를 덜렁 내놓은 사내도
꼬리가 반쯤 탄 개도 모두 납작해져 있다
안테나가 헐거워진 집을 단숨에 잡아당긴다
집은 그 흔한 뿌리도 구근도 매달지 않았다
뿌리까지 다 내놓고도 나무는
집과 길 밖에다 새를 감추어 두고 있다
집은 허공의 날개가 되었다
집은 여행 중이다

The House Is on Vacation

The windows and security grills are shut in a house where one road
meanders out like a herniated intestine
On the road a burning man and a dog slip out
The man with his genitals hanging loose
even the dog with a half-burned tail is flattened
The antenna pulls up the empty house in one breath
The house has no roots or dangling bulbs
Though the tree's roots hang loose
outside the house and road, it keeps a bird hidden
The house turns into wings in the air
The house is on vacation

검고 불룩한 TV와 나

1

1990년산 TV와
1968년산 나는 어둠 속에 있다

(낙타와 시간은 사막에 그냥 두고 왔다)

달빛이 흐릿하게 묻은
1990년산 TV와
1968년산 내 몸은 검고 불룩하다

1968년산 나는 쭈그리고 앉아
1990년산 TV를 영혼처럼 들여다본다

2

1990년산 TV와 1968년산 나. 생산년도가 있는 것들.
제품번호가 붙여진 것들. 뜨거운 것들. 뭉클거리는 것들.
어쩌자고 내 몸속에서 꺼지지 않는 TV. 내 몸에게로 나를
송출하는 TV. 난지도 TV. 검고 불룩한 달 속의 물. 물속
의 몸. 열 수 없는 우물. 끌 수 없는 창. 어둠 속에 웅크리
고 있는 것들. 퍼덕거리는 것들

Dark and Bulging TV and Me

I

A TV from 1990 and
my body made in 1968 are inside a darkness

(a camel and time were left in a desert)

Moonlight vaguely tainted
the TV from 1990 and
my body from 1968 is dark and bulging

In 1968 I crouch
I peer like a ghost into the 1990 TV

2

The TV from 1990 and my body from 1968. Products with the
year they were made. Products with serial numbers. Products that
scald. Bulky products. Somehow the TV in my body won't turn off.
The TV broadcasts me to my body. TV dumped at the Nanji Island
landfill. Water inside the dark, bulging TV. Body underwater. The
well that can't be opened. The window that can't be turned off.
Things crouching in the darkness. Fluttering things.

3

내 몸속엔 20년 전 죽었다는, 썩지 않는 풍문의 아버지가 하나.
녹슨 삽 하나. 녹슨 눈물 한 방울. 고철로 구겨진 발 둘. 뼈와
쇠숟가락. 모래로 채워진 산양의 눈 둘. 깨진 거울. 비닐봉지.
지는 별. 지는 봄. 지는 봄의 등에 걸린 지는 해. 수평선을 넘지
못하는 해 속의 물. 돌밭. 한밤의 검고 불룩한 TV. TV에 병렬
케이블로 연결된 무덤이 둘. 또 둘

3

Inside me is the father of an indisputable rumor, not decomposing, who has been dead 20 years. Rusted spade. Rusted teardrop. Pair of feet dented by scrap metal. Bone and brass spoon. Goat's eyes full of sand. Shattered mirror. Plastic bag. Shooting star. The end of spring. The last drum of spring caught on the setting sun. The water inside the sun can't cross the horizon. A field of stones. Midnight's dark and bulging TV. Two rows of graves are connected to the TV with cables. Two more.

뿌리들 1

모니터 뒤에 숨어
핀 돌단풍의 흰 꽃이
하나, 둘, 셋, 넷……
아니 모니터가 가리고
있던 아니 내가
가리고 있던 내 눈이
가리고 있던 돌단풍의
흰 꽃이 하나 둘 셋
넷……

Roots 1

Hidden behind the monitor
Crimson Fans white flowers bloom
one, two, three, four . . .
no, the monitor was blocking
no, I was covering no, my eyes
were hiding the blossoms
one two three
four . . .

뿌리들 2

집 속에 몸을 넣고 있으면 자꾸
몸이 집 밖으로 흘러넘친다

집 속에는 플러그 하나가
사리처럼 남아
사방을 두리번거리고 있다

Roots 2

If you leave your body inside a house
your body will keep spilling out

there's one plug in the house
it stays like a crystal bead
searching all over the place

뿌리들 3

쉴 새 없이 봉분의 밑을 파 들어갔다
흙들이 예리하게 절단되었다
뻣뻣한 넝쿨의 공기가 뻗어나갔다
어둠이 지문처럼 우글거렸다

거역할 수 없는 이 냄새
느릿느릿 배어나오는

하나의 돌이 열리는 소리
공기가 오래된 뚜껑처럼 멈추어 있다
돌은 사방에서 오래 닫혀진다
낯선 발들은 오래 가려진다
낯선 발들은 서로를 문처럼 들여다본다

빛처럼 작고 단단한 구멍이 있다 두개골마다
빛처럼 뽑혀져 나온 금속선이 있다 두개골마다
조여지지 않는 뼈를 흔들고 있다 장애물처럼

낯선 발들은 낯선 발들을 밟고 있다
낯선 발들을 화환처럼 들고 있다
공기가 오래된 뚜껑처럼 멈추어 있다
낯선 발들을 식빵처럼 뜯어 먹고 있다

Roots 3

I dig into the base of the burial mound
The soil is finely shaved
The air in the stiff vines splayed out
The darkness swarms like fingerprints

This irresistible creeping
stench

The sound of a single stone opens
The air is still like an old lid
The stones are kept closed
Unfamiliar feet are long hidden
Unfamiliar feet stare into each other like doors

There's a hole in every skull as tiny and hard as light
There's a wire in every skull pulled out as light
shaking skulls that can't be squeezed like an obstruction

Unfamiliar feet step on unfamiliar feet
holding them like they're wreaths
The air is still like an old lid
I gnaw on my unfamiliar feet like they're bread

거역할 수 없는 이 냄새
수맥을 봉쇄해버린

단정한 나무의 배선
복사되는 배선

하강할 수 있음
계속
내려가시오

거역할 수 없는 이 포르말린 냄새
썩지 않는 죽음
아래는 아주 넓고 깊다

This irresistible stench
seals off the ground water

The wires of a tidy tree
reproduce a circuit

You can go down
keep
going lower

This irresistible stench of formalin
unrotting death
the bottom so wide and deep

길

시간은 벽과 벽 사이에서 흘러넘치고 있습니다

어둠이 길들을 천천히 멍석처럼 말아갑니다

열었던 세계만큼 창들은 다시 세계를 닫습니다

고압선들이 허공 위로 툭툭 불거집니다

몸통만 남은 나무에 옷이 길게 늘어져 있습니다

한 여자가 이십 년을 살고 죽었습니다

4월생이었습니다

밤은 점점 가파르고

반쯤 남아 있는 길에서 고기 삶는 냄새가 진동하고 있습니다

Road

Time overflows between walls

Darkness rolls up the roads like a straw mat

Windows close the world as much as it was opened

Power lines turn red and stick out of the air

A shirt stretched onto a tree left with just its trunk

A woman lived twenty years and died

She was born in April

The night deepens

Halfway down the road the stench of boiling meat

오토바이

왕복 4차선 도로를 쭉 끌고
은색 오토바이가 굉음을 내며 질주한다
오토바이의 바퀴가 닿은 길이 팽창한다
길을 삼킨 허공이 꿈틀거린다
오토바이는 새처럼 끊긴 길을 좋아하고
4차선 도로는 허공에서도 노란 중앙선을 꽉 붙들고 있다

오토바이에 끌려가는 도로의 끝으로 아파트가 줄줄이 따라온다
뽑혀져 나온 아파트의 뿌리는 너덜너덜한 녹슨 철근이다
썩을 줄 모르는 길과 뿌리에서도 잘 삭은 흙냄새가 나고
사방에서 몰려든 햇빛들은 물을 파먹는다
오토바이는 새처럼 뿌리의 벼랑인 허공을 좋아하고
아파트 창들은 허공에서도 벽에 간 금을 필사적으로 붙잡고 있다

도로의 끝을 막고 있던 아파트가 딸려가자
모래들이 울부짖으며 몰려온다 낙타들이 발을 벗어들고 달려온다
그러나 낙타들은 우는 모래 밖으로 나가본 적이 없고
모래들은 울부짖으면서도 아파트 그림자에 자석처럼 철컥철컥 붙어간다
모래도 뜨겁기는 마찬가지여서
오토바이는 허공에 전 생애를 성냥처럼 죽 그으며 질주한다
아파트는 허공에서도 제 그림자를 다시 꾸역꾸역 삼키고 있다

Motorcycle

Straight to the end of a four-lane highway
A silver motorcycle speeds along with a roar
The road expands as the motorcycle's tires make contact
The air, swallowing the road, wriggles
The motorcycle, like a bird, delights in the dead-end road
The four-lane highway clings to the yellow center line, even up in the air

The motorcycle drags rows of apartments to the dead end
The apartments' rusted roots trail behind
The highway and roots aren't rotted but still give off the scent
        of lush decay
Light rushing in from all directions devours water
The motorcycle, like a bird, enjoys the flowing air at the roots' end
The apartment windows clutch the cracks in the wall, even up in the air

As the apartment blocking the dead end gets dragged away
The sand swarms in, wailing, camels take off their hooves and lope
But the camels have never been outside the weeping sand
The wailing sand clicks like a magnet to the apartment's shadow
The sand burns as hot as the motorcycle
The motorcycle speeds through its previous life like a match struck
        in the air
Even up in the air the apartment again swallows its own shadow

길, 오토바이, 나이키

길은 계속해서 제 속에서 제 몸을 천천히 빼내고 있다
길은 미끈거린다 길에서는 늘 시간의 피비린내가 난다
길은 여기에 서서 멀리까지 간 제 몸을 그리워한다

오토바이는 계속해서 길 끝에서 길 끝으로 탈주한다
오토바이는 항문의 속도로 들끓는다 따가워 매워
오토바이는 길에서는 도저히 발을 떠올릴 수조차 없다

달리는 오토바이 위에서 몸은 계속해서 팽창하고 있다
두 발이 가까스로 남은 눈알처럼 허공을 더듬는다
빛 속에서 생겨난 그림자가 앙상하다
몸보다 커진 심장이 벌컥벌컥 시간의 고삐를 잡고 간다

*점점 심장은 저보다 커졌죠: 에밀리 디킨슨의 편지.

Road, Motorcycle, Nike

The road slowly keeps pulling its body from itself
The road is slippery. The road always reeks of time's blood
The road misses its body that's gone from here to way over there

The motorcycle keeps escaping from one end of the road to another
The motorcycle makes a ruckus speeding like an anus—it's prickly,
                    it's spicy
The motorcycle can't remember its feet on the road

The body on the motorcycle expands
Feet like barely remaining eyeballs grope the air
Thin shadows form inside the light
The gulping heart bigger than the body grasps time's reins

*My heart slowly grew bigger than me: Emily Dickinson's letter.

나이키 1

한 무리의 아이들이 자신들의 그림자가 달라붙어 있는 벽을 향해 뛰어
간다 입을 항문처럼 오므렸다 폈다 하며 두 다리를 번갈아 들었다 내
렸다 하며 뛰어간다 아이들의 그림자는 계속 벽을 밀고 있다 미끄러
져 내리지는 않는다 길들은 벽을 피해 양쪽으로 갈라진다 물렁한 벽
인 하늘이 녹아내린다 짓무른 길의 가랑이 속에서 그림자를 죽죽 늘이
며 아이들은 함성을 지르며 뛴다 함성과 발소리가 아이들 앞에 순식간
에 벽이 되어 선다 그러나 자궁을 찢고 나온 적이 있는 아이들은 속도
를 줄이지 않는다 아이들의 몸에 하늘이 고름처럼 엉겨붙는다 아이들
의 몸이 점점 더 불어난다 아이들은 자신들이 세운 벽을 뚫고 다시 벽
을 세우고 다시 뚫는다 아이들은 진득진득하고 달콤하다 몸에서 떨어
져본 적이 없는 그림자도 벽을 계속 밀어낸다 벽 위까지 튕겨 오르던
그림자는 벽을 뛰어넘지는 못한다 그러나 그림자는 벽 속으로 스미지
않는다 높고 가파른 벽 너머는 보이지 않는다 아이들은 벽 너머가 보
이지 않기 때문에 뛴다

Nike 1

A group of kids run toward the wall where their shadows are stuck. Their lips pucker like anuses and their legs pump up and down as they run. The kids' shadows keep pushing themselves against the wall. They don't slip down. Roads split to either side to avoid the wall. The soft wall of sky melts down. In the festering crotch of the road, the kids stretch their shadows as they scream and run. Their screams and stomping turns into a wall in front of them. But the children who had once been torn from a womb don't slow down. The sky clings to the kids' bodies like pus. Their bodies start to bloat. They tear through the wall they built and rebuild the wall and tear through it again. They become sticky and sweet. The shadows that have never been separated from their bodies keep pushing up against the wall. The shadows jumping toward the top of the wall can't clear it. The shadows can't seep into the wall. Nothing is visible beyond the sheer wall. The kids keep running because they can't see beyond the wall.

나이키 2

한 아이가 달려간다
오른팔은 땅을 향해 떨어지고 있고
(오른손은 손등을 보인 채)
왼팔은 팔꿈치가 살짝 안으로 꺾인 채 올라가 있고
(왼손은 손바닥이 보인 채)
오른쪽 다리는 앞으로 들려 있고
(오른발은 신발 뒤꿈치가 땅에 닿아 있고)
왼쪽 다리는 뒤쪽으로 높이 올라가 있고
(왼발은 허공에 들려 신발 밑창이 다 보이고)
단추를 목까지 채운 몸통이
LPG통처럼 덩그마니 가운데 떠 있고
땅바닥으로 그림자가 가스처럼 새어나오고
고개를 약간 쳐든 얼굴은
하늘 쪽으로 둥둥 떠간다

여섯 조각으로 해체된 아이
발은 나이키가 꼭 조이고 있다

Nike 2

One child runs
The child's right arm drops to the ground
(glimpse the back of his right hand)
The child's left elbow bends slightly and lifts
(glimpse his left palm)
His right leg moves forward
(his right shoe touches the ground)
His left leg pushes off behind him
(the sole of his left shoe entirely in view)
He is buttoned up to the neck
like an LPG gas tank floating by
The child's shadow escapes from the ground like gas
The child's face tilts slightly upward
floats up to the sky

The child fractured into six stop-motion frames
Nike tightens around his feet

나이키 - 절벽

와와와 아이들이 폭우가 쏟아지는 광장으로 뛰쳐나온다 여기는 지구
다 달걀 속이다 세찬 빗줄기는 위에서 아래로 내리꽂힌다 허공에서 바
닥으로 쏟아지며 전속력으로 벽을 쌓는 순간 전속력으로 벽을 무너뜨
린다 콘크리트 바닥은 무너진 세계를 받아들이지 않는다 무너진 벽을
탕탕 튕기며 아이들은 아래에서 위로 뛰어오른다 뜨거운 것에 데인 듯
이 한자리에서 펄쩍펄쩍 뛰어오른다 아이들의 발은 벽을 폈다 접었다
한다 발에 벽이 들어 있다 아이들은 젖은 몸으로 빗속에서 뛰어오른
다 아이들이 뛰는 곳 말고는 사방이 점점 더 어두워진다 아이들 발의
사방이 어두워진다 한곳을 계속 뛰기 때문에 발아래가 깊어진다 깊은
것은 어둡다 야생이다 아이들의 발은 길의 끝이다 길의 시작이다 발
소리가 깊어진다 절벽이 깊어진다 아니 절벽이 솟아오른다 절벽은 미
어져내리는 깊이다 다시 솟구쳐오르는 날개다 온몸에 빗줄기를 화살
처럼 꽂고 아이들은 숨구멍 하나 없는 하늘과 땅 사이에서 뛰어오른
다 깔깔거리며 몸 밖으로 뚫린 눈으로 몸 안을 뚫으며 제자리에서 뛰
어오르고 또 뛰어오른다 빗줄기는 절벽 아래까지 단숨에 내리꽂힌다
그 소리도 깊다 야생이다 아이들의 발소리는 몸 안에 벽을 쌓는 순간
벽을 무너뜨린다 내출혈로 절벽이 들끓는다

Nike—Edge

Wow-wow-wow! In the heavy downpour, children run to the square. This world is the inside of an egg. Torrential rainfall. It pours downward at such an alarming rate that it becomes a wall of rain, yet in a matter of seconds is dismantled. The concrete floor is impervious to the collapsing world. The children bounce against the collapsed wall, bang, bang, as they leap up. They jump up and down as if on fire. Their feet fold and unfold the wall. The wall is embedded in their feet. The rain-soaked children keep jumping. It grows dark everywhere except for where the children are leaping. The ground around their feet grows darker. The ground deepens because they keep jumping in one place. The depth is dark. It's wild. The children's feet are the end of the road. The beginning of the road. Their stomping intensifies. The edge sharpens. No, the edge shoots upward. The edge is a plummeting depth. It soars again as if on wings. The children's bodies are pierced with arrows and they leap up, giggling, between the breathless sky and ground. They leap outside of their bodies, outside of their eye sockets, piercing their bodies, they leap in place. The rain strikes to the very bottom of the edge in a single breath. The sound of the striking rain is deep. It's wild. The moment the children's footsteps build walls inside their bodies, they tear them down. The edge swarms in a hemorrhage.

아파트에서 1

한 남자의 두 손이 한 여자의
양쪽 어깨를 잡더니 앞뒤로
마구 흔들었다 남자의 손이
여자의 살 속으로 쑥쑥 빠졌다
여자가 제 몸속에 뒤엉켜 있는
철사를 잡아 빼며 울부짖었다
소리소리 질렀다
여자의 몸에서 마르지 않은
시멘트 냄새가 났다
꽃 피고 새가 울었다

At the Apartment 1

The man's two hands got a hold
of her shoulders and shook violently
His hands sank into her flesh
She wailed as she yanked
a twisted wire from her body
She screamed and screamed
Her body smelled
like wet cement
A flower bloomed, a bird cried

아파트에서 2

사람들이 층층의 정육점에서 뛰쳐나온다
갈고리가 몸의 여기저기에 박힌 채였다
몸의 지퍼를 올리지도 못한 채였다
그림자가 몸을 만들기도 전에
몸의 사방에 불빛이 대못처럼 박힌다
뛰어가는 그들의 몸속에서
쇠붙이끼리 부딪치는 소리가 난다
쇠붙이끼리 절거덕 붙는 소리가 난다

At the Apartment 2

Lines of people pour from the butcher shop
Hooks embedded through their bodies
they can't zip their bodies up
Before the shadow makes a body
light is embedded in the body like nails
In their running bodies
the sound of metal knocking together
the sound of metal clicking together

아파트에서 3

늙은 여자 여럿이
한낮의 아파트 주차장에 쭈그리고 앉아
그림자를 낳는다
어느 여자는 진득진득한 돌을 낳는다

At the Apartment 3

Several old women
crouch in the apartment parking lot at midday
giving birth to shadows
One woman gives birth to a sticky stone

밤의 놀이터

한밤중 놀이터에 말이 있었다

모래 속에는 몸통만 남은 말이 다섯 마리 있었다

희고 검고 파랗고 노랗고 붉은 말이 있었다

머리를 관통한 쇠막대기가 함께 있었다

내륙 산간에 폭설이 쏟아지고 있었다

하늘로부터 온 신의 메시지는 모래 위에 새겨지지 않았다

Night's Playground

Late at night there were horses in the playground

Just the torsos of five horses remain in the sand

The horses were white, black, blue, yellow, and red

Metal rods penetrated their heads

Heavy snow fell over the mountainside

There was no message from heaven recorded in the sand

소금 사막

세상을 향해 잘못 열린 관 같은 소파에 한 남자가 몸을 웅크리고 누워 있다 동쪽의 어둠을 끌고 온 커튼과 서쪽의 어둠을 끌고 온 커튼 사이가 비명처럼 벌어진다 한줄기 빛이 찢어진 생살에 뿌려지는 소금처럼 스며든다 오래된 적막이 쓴 물을 뱉어내며 쩍쩍 갈라진다 등을 보인 채 모은 두 다리를 가슴 쪽으로 끌어당기고 있는 남자는 꾸물꾸물 생겨나고 있는 태아 같아서 버석거리며 증발해가는 소금 사막의 물기 같아서 제 몸을 파먹어 들어가던 어둠이 남자의 등속을 파고든다 그곳에 살그머니 고인다 남자의 사방에서 벽들이 질주한다 제 몸에서 빛이 새어나오는지도 모르고 어둠은 내내 질려 있다

Salt Desert

On a couch like an incorrectly sealed coffin open to the world a man curls up. The gap between the curtain that drags in the darkness of the east and the curtain that drags in the darkness of the west widens in a scream. A ray of light gets absorbed like sprinkled salt over torn flesh. Old silence spits out bitter water as it splinters. With his back to me and legs pulled into his chest, he wriggles like a growing fetus. He rustles like desert saltwater drying up. The darkness gnawing on its own body is gnawing on his back. The darkness quietly gathers in the hole of his back. The walls around him scamper. The darkness is dead tired, unaware of the light leaking out from itself.

거울이 얼굴을 뜯어 먹는다

거울 속에서 나는 마르고 긴 빵을 뜯어 먹는다 나는 밤을 기다리고 있다 거울 속은 해가 지지 않는다 하늘은 여전히 어떤 몸도 닿을 수 없는 곳으로 제 피를 몰고 번져간다 거울이 어두워지지 않자 이번에는 순서를 바꾸어 빵이 내 얼굴을 뜯어 먹는다 읽을 수 없는 꿈이야 수천의 시간이 타고 있는 만장이야 마르고 뻣뻣한 내 살을 죽죽 뜯어 먹는다 파헤쳐진 내 얼굴 속에는 씹다 만 별의 몸 낙타의 발자국 나사못 맨드라미 씨앗 오전 10시35분 잘린 숨 그러나 처음 보는 시간의 피를 묻힌 거울은 소란스러워지지 않고 붙잡을 곳 없는 거울의 암벽으로 최초의 그림자가 생겨나고 있는 맨드라미 씨앗이 먼저 기어오른다 어둠이 차오르지 않아도 대지의 시간이 다시 시작되고 있다

The Mirror Gnaws on My Face

I gnaw on a baguette in the mirror. I wait for night. The sun in the mirror won't set. The sky keeps spreading its blood beyond the places that bodies can't reach. The mirror won't darken. This time it switches around. The baguette gnaws on my face. It's a dream I can't interpret. Thousands of hours burning inside the abyss. The baguette gnaws away at my dry and stiff flesh. Inside my dug-up face: a half-chewed star's body, a camel's hoofprint, a nail, a cockscomb seed, 10:35 AM, my breath cut short. The first time I look into the mirror, smeared with the blood of time, unfussy and with no place to hold, the first shadow of a cockscomb seed climbs the mirror's rockface. Even if the darkness won't brim to the top, the earth's time begins anew.

얼굴이 그립다

얼굴이 거울을 열고 들어간다 나도 따라 들어가려고 하니 얼굴은 어느새 거울을 잠가버린다 거울로 들어가는 문을 찾는다 거울은 미끄럽고 태연하다 구름무늬가 양각된 타일이 얼굴의 사방에 붙는다 얼굴은 벽의 시간이 된다 나는 이제 막 내 등까지 도착한 오늘의 밤에 기댄다 밤은 나를 뒤적이지 않는다 내가 밤을 버릴 수 없는 것은 내가 공포이기 때문이다 공포는 사랑이며 공포는 껴안을 수밖에 없다는 것을 아는지 거울 속의 얼굴이 나 대신 입을 벌린다 그곳의 밤이 얼굴을 한 줄 한 줄 벗겨낸다 맨살이 새잎 나고 꽃필 것처럼 깜깜하다 거울로 들어가는 문을 찾지 못해 내게는 오늘의 밤이 계속된다 얼굴이 낯설어진다 내가 거울 밖으로 고개를 다 돌리기도 전에 거울 속의 얼굴이 뒤통수를 보인다 사랑은 공포여서 나는 거울 밖으로 걸어나온다 몇 걸음도 걷지 못하고 나를 두고 거울의 밤 속으로 사라진 얼굴이 벌써 그립다

I Miss My Face

My face opens the mirror and goes inside. I follow but my face locks up the mirror. I look for the door in the mirror. The mirror is slippery and calm. Cloud-engraved tiles stick to each side of my face. My face becomes time on the wall. I lean against the night that reaches behind me. Night doesn't rifle through me. I can't give up the night because I'm a horror. A horror is love, so there's nothing to do but embrace it. The mirror knows this, so my face in the mirror opens its mouth on my behalf. The night inside the mirror peels my face line by line. My bare flesh sprouts new leaves and grows dark as if it's about to bear blooms. Since I can't find the door, the night ceases to end. My face becomes unfamiliar to me. Before I turn away from the mirror, the back of my head appears. Love is a horror, so I walk out from the mirror. Short a few steps I miss my face vanished into the mirror's night.

얼굴이 달린다

거울 속에서 얼굴이 달린다 가도 가도 끝없는 거울이다 거울의 풍경이
바뀌지 않는 것은 안이 온통 사막이기 때문이다 사막은 쉴 새 없이 모래
의 기억을 바꾼다 사막은 어디나 한가운데여서 절정이어서 얼굴은 거울
과 함께 뜨거워진다 시간의 컨테이너인 얼굴에서 공기가 빠져나간다 눈
코 입이 다 번진다 시간의 소용돌이가 된다 얼굴을 삼키지도 토하지도
않는 거울이 점점 새파래진다 거울 속의 얼굴이 멈춰 있는 것은 너무 빠
른 속도로 얼굴이 달리고 있기 때문이다 얼굴 속에 어긋나야만 걸을 수
있는 오른발과 왼발처럼 물과 어둠이 있다

My Face Runs

My face runs inside the mirror. The mirror is endless. The landscape never shifts because inside the mirror is all desert. The desert keeps shifting the sand's memory. Wherever it is the desert stays in the center, the peak, so both the face and mirror heat up. Air escapes from my face, a container of time. My eyes, nose, and lips spread into a whirlpool of time. The mirror that never swallows or throws up my face turns blue. My face is frozen in the mirror because it's running too fast. Inside my face there's water and darkness like left and right feet that only walk if they cross in the opposite direction.

거울이 달아난다

거울에 들어가 거울을 생각하면 거울이 달아난다 출구를 어떻게 알았는지 내 얼굴과 벽만 그대로 두고 거울 밖으로 떠간다 무거웠던 것은 자작극을 벌이던 것은 거울이 아니라 얼굴과 벽이다 거울이 달아난 곳에서의 벽과 얼굴은 서로의 공기를 밀어낸다 얼굴은 뻑뻑하다 벽은 벽의 시간에 더 바싹 몸을 붙이며 숨막힌다 거울이 사라져간 방향에서 몰려온 길이 얼굴을 잡아당긴다 대지가 되기에는 나는 어둠이 부족하다 드넓은 풀밭이 되기에는 나는 절망을 모른다 얼굴은 길을 받아들이지 않는 힘으로 단단해진다 막힌 얼굴과 막힌 벽 사이에서 길들이 테니스공처럼 튕겨진다 얼굴을 만날 수 없는 얼굴은 자꾸만 제 안을 파고 들어간다 점점 멀어지는 곳에서 발이 울고 있다

The Mirror Runs Away

If I go inside the mirror thinking of the mirror, it runs away. Somehow it finds an exit and floats out of the mirror, leaving behind the wall and my face. What weighs heavy on me is the fact it was the wall and the face scheming a plot and not the mirror. In the place where the mirror runs off to, the face and the wall push out each other's air. The face is stiff. The wall clings closer to time, gasping. The roads swarm in from where the mirror has disappeared and pull on my face. I lack the darkness to become earth. I don't know the despair to become a wide patch of grass. The face stiffens from exerting strength, blocking roads. Between my blocked face and wall, the roads bounce along like tennis balls. The face that can never meet a face keeps digging into itself. My feet cry in the widening distance.

거울을 위하여

거울: 내가 들여다보면 내가 사라져버리는
벽 또는 언어

살그머니 들어갈 것 두리번거리지 말 것 의
심하지 말 것 거울 속으로 손을 뻗지 말 것
뒤돌아보지 말 것

어제의 시간과 내일의 시간이 거울로 걸
어 들어와 조우한다 복받쳐올라 서로 아무
말 못한다 쓰다듬지도 못한다 한없이
쳐다보고만 있다 거울을 보면 입을 다물게
되는 이유다

거울을 들여다본다 시간이 움찔한다 한 두
번 그러는 것도 아닌데 매번 그런다

거울 속에서 내 얼굴이 천천히 흘러가고 있
다 나는 꽃잎도 아닌데 더욱 나는 불빛도
아닌데

For the Mirror

Mirror: The wall or language.
When I look into it, I vanish.

Enter quietly. Don't look around. Don't question.
Don't spread your hand into the mirror. Don't
look back.

Yesterday's hour and tomorrow's hour enter
the mirror and run into each other. They're too
stunned to say anything. They don't touch each
other. They just stare. This is why our lips stay
shut when we look in the mirror.

Though it's not the first time I look in the mirror,
time always flinches.

Though I'm not a petal or a light, I slowly drift in
the mirror.

흐르는 것들은 제 안에 골짜기를 감추고 있
어 어둠 속에는 어둠이 구름 속에는 구름이
모래 속에는 모래가 씨앗 속에는 씨앗이 허
공 속에는 허공이 거울 속에는 거울이 얼굴
속에는 얼굴이 들어 있다

사람들은 종종 타인의 얼굴에 시선을 자석
처럼 붙이고 따라가며 구경한다 시간의 창
이기 때문이다 사람들은 자신의 얼굴을 볼
때는 멈칫한다 시간의 벽이기 때문이다

질주하는 몸은 공포로 가득 찬 몸이다 거울
속으로 달려가면 거울 끝에 벽이 있다 질주
하던 몸은 날계란처럼 터진다

사람들은 눈앞에 보이는 벽 때문에 바로 뒤
의 벽을 떠올리지 못한다 진짜 벽을 감추기
위한 거울의 위장술이다 거울은 진화한다

거울을 스칠 때마다 얼굴이 베인다 거울에
베인 내 얼굴에는 시간이 핏물처럼 스민다

거울의 꿈은 제 내부를 온전하게 텅 비우는
것이다 꿈은 이루어지지 않을 때까지만 꿈
인 것이어서 거울은 계속 실존한다

The things that drift have a valley hidden inside.
Darkness inside darkness, cloud inside cloud, sand
inside sand, seed inside seed, void inside void,
mirror inside mirror, face inside face.

People are drawn like a magnet to other people's
faces. Because others' faces are windows of time.
People hesitate at seeing their own faces. Because
their reflections are a wall of time.

The speeding body is full of fear. It rushes inside
the mirror to the end of the wall. The speeding
body bursts against it like a raw egg.

People can't see the wall behind the wall right in
front of them. The mirror puts on a disguise to
hide the real wall. The mirror is evolving.

Every time I brush past the mirror, my face gets
cut. Time seeps like blood into my cut face.

The dream of the mirror will drain my insides.
A dream is only a dream while unattained, so the
mirror continues to exist.

벽 속에서 거울이 투명하게 썩어간다 거울
속의 나도 투명하게 썩어간다

거울: 내가 밖으로 나와도 내가 사라지지
않는 내가 갇혀서 끓고 있는 진창

Inside the wall, the clear mirror rots away. The transparent I inside the mirror also rots.

Mirror: I emerge from it without vanishing. I am trapped in boiling sludge.

사랑 또는 두 발

내 발 속에 당신의 두 발이 감추어져 있다
벼랑처럼 감추어져 있다
달처럼 감추어져 있다
울음처럼 감추어져 있다

　　어느 날 당신이 찾아왔다
　　열매 속에서였다
　　거울 속에서였다
　　날개를 말리는 나비 속에서였다
　　공기의 몸 속에서였다
　　돌멩이 속에서였다

내 발 속에 당신의 두 발이 감추어져 있다
당신의 발자국은 내 그림자 속에 찍히고 있다
당신의 두 발이 걸을 때면
어김없이 내가 반짝인다 출렁거린다
내 온몸이 쓰라리다

Love or Feet

Your feet are hidden inside my feet
hidden like a precipice
hidden like the moon
hidden like tears

One day you came to visit
inside fruit
inside a mirror
inside a butterfly drying its wings
inside the body of air
inside a stone

Your feet are hidden inside my feet
your footprints stamped inside my shadow
When your feet step away
without fail I twinkle and slosh
my whole body aches

거울의 춤

나비는 봄의 방향으로 날아오고 있고
낙타는 사막의 방향으로 걸어가고 있고
인간은 허공의 방향으로 번지고 있고
나는 거울의 방향으로 뛰어가고 있다

낙타가 가는 곳은 모두 사막이고
(낙타는 모래를 따라가고 모래는 별을 따라가고
별은 낙타의 발바닥에 굳은살로 박히고)
나비가 오는 곳은 모두 봄이고
(날개는 늘 싹트고 있는 눈이다)
내가 가는 곳은 길이고 거울이고
(시간은 슬픔을 한 방울도 흘리지 않는다 그러나
시간은 슬픔 한 방울로 굴러간다)
인간이 지금 가는 곳은 허공이다
(허공에 경을 새겨넣는 손들
원본이 존재하지 않아 흐르는 경문들)

그러므로
봄이며
봄의 방향이며
봄의 춤인
나비여

The Mirror's Dance

The butterfly flies in the direction of spring
The camel walks in the direction of the desert
The human spreads in the direction of the void
I run in the direction of the mirror

Everywhere the camel goes is a desert
(The camel follows the sand, the sand follows the stars,
the stars are studded and callous under the camel's hooves)
Everywhere the butterfly flies is spring
(The wings always blossoming with eyes)
Everywhere I go is a road and a mirror
(Time doesn't shed a single drop of sorrow, but then
time rolls away like a drop of sorrow)
Everywhere the human goes is a void
(Hands that imprint hours in the void,
the original doesn't exist, so they flow like prayers)

Therefore
it's spring
it's the direction of spring
it's the spring dance
it's the butterfly

그러므로
허공이며
허공의 방향이며
허공의 춤인
인간이여

그러므로
사막이며
사막의 방향이며
사막의 춤인
낙타여

그러므로
길의 방향이며 거울의 방향이며
길이며 거울의 춤인
나여

Therefore
it's the void
it's the direction of the void
it's the dance of the void
it's the human

Therefore
it's the desert
it's the direction of the desert
it's the desert dance
it's the camel

Therefore
it's the direction of the road, the mirror
it's the road, the mirror dance
it's me

Translators' Notes

Since her poems debuted in 1992, Yi Won has been renowned in Korea for her avant-garde modernist poetry. Her work is appreciated for its paradigm shifts about the information age and digital civilization. Yi Won often cites Edward Hopper's paintings as deeply influential, calling them works of the future. "Poetry should have both sharpness and sensitivity in the realm of foretelling," she says. "This is one of the reasons for the existence of art." Yi Won's poetic interests focus on the point at which a movement is about to happen across South Korea's landscape, citing chaos theory, where, within complex systems around the globe, she breaks open feedback loops that define our interconnectedness, our universality. She says, "The movement of Korea is also aligned with the movement of the world."

> People everywhere
> walk with plugs suspended from their bodies
> charged by the world's rage
>
> "On the Street"

Yi Won's predecessors of Korean women feminist poets include Kim Hyesoon, whose poems have served to protect and strengthen junior women poets since they were first published in 1979. In recent years, worldwide attention has turned to Korean women's feminist poetry. Yi Won says, "Korean women poets always wrote poetry with a clear perspective. Feminism has emerged to become more visible through social issues. [. . .] Feminist poets in Korean society provide the imagination to design the ideal future through language. It makes you dream. Poetic suggestions and poetic smudges can help Korean society to mature." These poetic smudges are important to the language of poetry, especially for Korean women poets. "Korean women poets did not write poetry only in the language of resistance. They wrote poems beyond the limits of feminism." Yi Won is a successor of such Korean women's poetry. She says, "I grew up in a more relaxed social setting than [Kim Hyesoon]. Personally, I grew up in a freer atmosphere. Indeed, I am free to write poetry away from the distinction between women/men, beings/objects. It is a world that I meet as a being which even I cannot name. An image I cannot name." Yi Won is interested in freeing distinctions. Instead of speaking clearly and directly, she aims for an openness in her imagery. Instead of differences, she questions the place in which those differences meet, overlap, and expand reality. Yi Won writes poems with rich layers of language that are delicate, brave, and inclusive, with depths that cannot be singularly defined.

> When I caress the package
> I can feel its hard edges
> Ah! I didn't think a coffin could be so warm
>
> "Your Package"

Yi Won does not define herself except in these terms: "I have the gaze of a being, which is important in the perspective as a poet." She is continuously inspired through art exhibits and books. In her twenties and thirties, she was drawn toward George Segal, Francis

Bacon, and Robert Frank. A central feature of her work is how she sees the world through images rather than meaning. "This feature makes me want to make my poetic language imagery newer and stranger," Yi Won says. The feature of newness and strangeness can be seen in her poems about houses, mirrors, motorcycles, and roads, among others. "The irony of the closest thing being the most unfamiliar seems to provide an unfamiliar and familiar image at the same time. I'm interested in questions such as whether what I see is true or not or whether what I see of myself is really me."

> I put my head on display at Ilsan Market, but after several days no one bought it
>
> I put my head up for auction online but got a notification that when you click my head an hourglass appears, a loading error
>
> "Self-Portrait"

As a teacher, Yi Won focuses on having her students create new perspectives. "One more point of view is like having more eyes." Yi Won gives her students more eyes. She wants them to see the things that are visible and invisible at the same time, to understand these movements as both vertical and horizontal networks. Nowadays, Yi Won asks herself two fundamental questions: "Do you never know the beauty you've never seen?" and "Is it beautiful to love something you've never known?"

One of the major challenges in translating Yi Won is the question of how to translate what is both visible and invisible. Yi Won's language is multitudinous, ever expanding. Her language refuses clear borders, and like a gravitational field, its revolving force merely lessens as you travel farther from its center. This is embodied in such poems as "Postcard," in which daffodils "open up their universe" as the speaker writes down an address, and zip codes waver and break apart. As the poem unfurls, the images begin to seep through their edges. Yi Won's poems, at their core, resist translation. Lauded as a poet who combines ancient Buddhist meditations on the human condition with the language of commerce and technology, she presses the limits of meaning through syntax in order to deconstruct and reconstruct. In the original text, the prose poems "Time and a Plastic Bag" and "Tick, Tick, Tick, Tick" imbue the humble comma, borrowed like most punctuation from Western traditions, with the power to disrupt time and space, cadence and grammar, which in turn encumbers an accurate rendering into English. Yet even that resistance to translation is important to keep in her poems in order to preserve the decibel of an image, such as the onomatopoeic title of "Tick, Tick, Tick, Tick" or the violent portrayal of time leaning against a tree "with one leg cut off, at the knee . . ." How, then, does one make visible the invisible from one language to the next in a text that resists translation? In a style of Korean that hurtles toward and away from the reader, the translation must seek to be a force against norms within English. Where English requires subject and verb, specific pronouns, or punctuation, Korean omits or circumvents them. In either direction, the translation becomes simultaneously a radical departure and radical arrival. Instead of seeing, feeling deeply into the unnamable abyss. Through uncertainty, allowing something to surface akin to language.

For her readers in English, Yi Won hopes we might find "a common language in another language." Of this delicate universality, she says, "There is a landscape of Earth that human beings make common." This landscape is where her poems reside, a place of both compatibility and conflict, not of dichotomy but of coexistence.

Acknowledgments

We are grateful to Don Mee Choi and the American Literary Translators Association's Emerging Translator Mentorship Program, LTI-Korea, and Harvard's Sunshik Min Endowment for the Advancement of Korean Literature for making the publication of this book possible. Thank you to Christopher Mattison, Leora Zeitlin, J. Kates, and everyone at Zephyr Press for their guidance and encouragement.

We are indebted to the community of Korean and Korean American women poets for their inspired work and scholarship. We owe the community of translators for their constant support. *AGNI, Asymptote; Chicago Review; Denver Quarterly; The Margins, the digital publication of the Asian American Writers' Workshop; Poetry Daily; Puerto del Sol;* and *Waxwing Literary Journal* have published some poems that appear in the collection. Our families and friends have carried us through the years.

Yi Won has given us "more eyes" to know the beauty we've never seen and to love the things we've never known.

Contributors

E. J. Koh is the author of the memoir *The Magical Language of Others* (Tin House Books, 2020), winner of the Pacific Northwest Book Award, and the poetry collection *A Lesser Love* (Louisiana State University Press, 2017), winner of the Pleiades Press Editors Prize for Poetry. Her poems, translations, and stories have appeared in *Boston Review, Los Angeles Review of Books, Slate,* and *World Literature Today.* Koh is the recipient of fellowships from the American Literary Translators Association, Kundiman, and MacDowell, and she was longlisted for the PEN Open Book Award. She earned her MFA at Columbia University for Creative Writing and Literary Translation. She is a PhD candidate at the University of Washington in Seattle for English Language and Literature on Korean and Korean American literature, history, and film.

Marci Calabretta Cancio-Bello is the author of *Hour of the Ox* (University of Pittsburgh, 2016), which won the Donald Hall Prize for Poetry. Her work has appeared in *Best Small Fictions, Kenyon Review Online, Orion, The New York Times,* and been anthologized in *You Don't Have to Be Everything: Poems for Girls Becoming Themselves* (Workman Publishing, 2021), *Grabbed: Poets & Writers on Sexual Assault, Empowerment & Healing* (Beacon, 2020), and *Ink Knows No Borders: Poems on the Immigrant and Refugee Experience* (Seven Stories Press, 2019). The recipient of fellowships from the American Literary Translators Association and Kundiman, Cancio-Bello earned an MFA in Poetry from Florida International University, where she was a John S. and James L. Knight Foundation Fellow. She is the poetry coordinator for the Miami Book Fair.